Barricades in West

BARRICADES IN WEST HAMPSTEAD

Bernard Kops

HEARING EYE

FOR ERICA

Published Winter 1988/1989
© Copyright of the poems retained by Bernard Kops, 1988

ISBN 1 870841 04 2 (hardback edition)
ISBN 1 870841 05 0 (paperback edition)

Published by Hearing Eye
Box No. 1, 99 Torriano Avenue, London NW5
Printed by Aldgate Press, E1

Barricades in West Hampstead is published in an edition of 1,000 copies
of which 1-50 will be signed by the author.

Contents

Contents

BARRICADES IN WEST HAMPSTEAD

All my children talk to me.
More or less.
And I have loved the same woman
for thirty three years.
More or less.
I suppose you could call that success,
if you ignore the pain
of almost everything.
And what's more we've been together
and stayed sane.
More or less.
Yes!
Despite the encroaching endless mess;
the heartless conversions
that threaten to engulf West Hampstead,
I still maintain my ridiculous oasis.
And here sometimes even neighbours
manage to smile and nod.
And my granddaughter thinks I am a god.
Why am I such a lucky sod?
More or less.

NEWLYWED

When all the world was afternoons
that went on all the day,
our friends came round
to share our dreams,
and ate us out of house and home.
And so we moved away.

1955

BREAKDOWN

All night I dreamed I lay awake
and now the day goes rushing through.
Borrowed from darkness once again,
I find that I have lost myself.
I leave a small note on the table.
Dear Mum, O can U not C how ill I am?
Goodbye.
I rush out through the wallpaper
and walk along the crowded parchment.
Help! Help! Catch me, I'm falling. Hell —
Childcall   Birdflight
Down to the endless seas of the never
ending ending night.
The sediment of dusk falls
Into the husk of night.
A spider sleeps and dreams of silver.
Oh we are the fragments of a dream,
a dream that has no dreamer.

1949

THE SAD BOYS

The sad boys of the afternoon
are wandering through the town,
looking for some lonely girls
to lay their bodies down.

The sad boys sit around and croon
but never lose their frown;
no one comes and no one goes;
they watch the leaves twist down.

The sad boys of the afternoon
pull petals from the park,
then throw them at the dying sun
and stroll into the dark.

1957

SHALOM BOMB

I want a bomb, my own private bomb, my shalom bomb.
I'll test it in the morning, when my son awakes,
hot and stretching, smelling beautiful from sleep. Boom! Boom!

Come my son dance naked in the room.
I'll test it on the landing and wake my neighbours,
the masons and the whores and the students who live down- stairs.

Oh I must have a bomb and I'll throw open windows and
count down as I whizz around the living room,
on his bike, with him flying angels on my shoulder;
and my wife dancing in her dressing gown.
I want a happy family bomb, a do-it-yourself bomb,
I'll climb on the roof and ignite it there about noon.
My improved design will gong the world and we'll all eat lunch.

My pretty little bomb will play a daytime lullaby and
thank you bomb for now my son falls fast asleep.
My love come close, close the curtains, my lovely bomb, my darling.

My naughty bomb. Burst around us, burst between us, burst within us.

Light up the universe, then linger, linger
while the drone of the world recedes.

Shalom bomb

I want to explode the breasts of my wife.
and wake everyone,
to explode over playgrounds and parks, just as children
come from schools. I want a laughter bomb,
filled with sherbert fountains, licorice allsorts, chocolate kisses,
candy floss,
tinsel and streamers, balloons and fireworks, lucky bags,
bubbles and masks and false noses.

I want my bomb to sprinkle the earth with roses.
I want a one-man-band-bomb. My own bomb.

My live long and die happy bomb. My die peacefully of old age bomb,
in my own bed bomb.
My Om Mane Padme Aum Bomb, My Tiddly Om Pom Bomb.
My goodnight bomb, my sleeptight bomb,
my see you in the morning bomb.
I want my bomb, my own private bomb, my Shalom bomb.

1959

SKYMAN

My God I'm dead . . .
the young man said
when he saw his battered head
petalled on the crimson sand.
. . . oh Mother come and meet me now
and take my hand . . .
His body like a fountain played
along the empty esplanade.
A coca-cola sign winked on
and when the moon came he was gone.

1962

HACKNEY! SUNDAY! RAIN!

Hackney! Sunday! Rain! You know the sort of day.

Black empty trees against a desolate sky.
Expressionless people buying sad daffodils outside the hospital,
people unaccustomed to flowers except for births marriages and death.

So many people come into this place
and so many go out, you know how,
and have their first contact with the earth
in God knows how long.

And here my father is going to die.
I walk to his bed where he smiles at me
although he is already dead,
his milk-white eyes taking,
taking their last look at the world.
He moans, over and over again.
Why? Why am I here? I have no pain.

He has nothing now to tell us, we his gathered children.
A nondescript life sliding into oblivion,
a nobody going nowhere, becoming no-one,
like everyone.
Yet death brings his face distinction,
breeding tells and his skull showing through
is as good as anyone's.

Cancer! Whisper it! Do not let him hear.
Have you seen the doctor? Is there any hope?
What did the sister say? Someone said worse than him
lived for another year.
How long? How long? How long do you think it will take?

I look out of the window.
Who knows, perhaps he can outlast the world.
Haven't you noticed a sudden deterioration
in almost everything?

The body of the world seems to be wasting away,
the face and the heart and the brain seem to decay.
Yet we pray and hope or try to hope and pray,
try to remove the growth
to live for another day.

Guilty, that I am not; grieving, because I cannot,
I run out into the world,
try to whistle, try not to weep.

And quickly get the tube away . . .

1962

TRAIN RIDE

It rained last night but now
sun sweeps across green lawns.
Blackbirds rise out of yielding winter,
smoking earth waits for spring;
the sky with open arms is showing off.

Beside me is a lovely girl
with long dark hair.
The sun strikes the amber of her dreaming eyes,
where I am trapped like a prehistoric fly.
She smiles.
I must get to know her.
She is my wife.

1962

EAST AND WEST

The copywriter no-world.
The dead jerking incompletes,
the dance of death.
The party goers. The standing lost
with drink in their claws,
in the deserts of their smart flats.
The space sellers.

The armour of expression covering faces
vomiting indifference over the whole
of endless Kensington.

So cancer spreads. People die and burst.
Look! There goes another.
Cancer eats through the walls of their
stomachs, up their lungs,
into their throats,
into their mouths and conversation.

I must get away.
Have I time to fly?
To soar out of these sickening streets?
I must dream that I can escape,
into the arms of my family.
I must embrace the things that made me.

Now they bring their dead to the place of worship.
My family. They sit in rows,
nodding.
It is a building I soon remember.
Incised crumbling walls;
it will stand long after it falls.
So I walk with my praying shadows,
shake their hand.
In the stark stone arena of my play
I see the stoop of my sad father,
and run the other way.

And in that tight room of wailing,
tea handed out with tears and giggles;
pinched cheeks of young girl brides,
speeded up, broken. Buds blown before burst,
blown inward. And here am I, too big for
boots, handed down the evil eye.
Where do I belong?
Here among the washing tubs?

The old men congregate.
The women have a sense of tragic placing
along the Mile End waste,
crowded with ghosts of playing children.

Tell me I dream as I laugh and sing and scream.

I see the coil of sound leaving my numb mouth,
I snap off the spiral, the plume of sound,
shape it like a paper plane and hurl it into ground
just as my fat sisters take the stairs,
wave their hands so frequently as they climb into clouds.
Their white blobs of pink
flesh blowing in the dark sky.

This is the East, where we lived once.
Where we once loved. Before the West went up,
fell down, pulling the rest.
The West was my growing up. I grew from East to West.
But my feet still cling where I crawled out of the mud
bleeding,
and slithered the shores to Aldgate East.

But now the dead are laid down. Look. All my family.
All the members one by one. They carry each other,
each in turn.
The living carry the dead away and the dead carry
the living back again.

The old men in my mirror wail.
Their cries split the sky,
cause the thunder to crash and the earth
to heave and the trees to splinter and the
leaves to burn
and the stones to crack and the faces to burst, open.

The synagogue explodes.
Then, my grandfathers with the usual blood streaming
from their eyes, go down quietly under the great
chunks of rock.
And my temple is destroyed. Shot right through.
Night dies. The glass-stained earth.
I am now walking away, somewhat relieved
by the menacing fists of dawn.

At dawn . . . the world yawns. It's day. Day.
My wife sings. My children, born and unborn
play.
At night the worms nibble my dreams away.

1963

ERICA I WANT TO READ YOU SOMETHING

Annihilation is easier when you are lonely.
But a man who is past it,
who knows no hope, who fears,
who fears there is no reason,
is known to me.

That man knows no order, no purpose,
but only knows a casual shape that has become
familiar.
Yet that man does not sing through me.

It all ends in death.
But when you love someone or detach yourself
from your own sadness,
this loss of life is more felt.

When you have a wife in bed,
a wife warm and passionate and beautiful,
when you are in her and she in you
completely,
when your shadows and personalities merge,
what then?

What of the coming loss, one way or another?

Or can the shape of infinite endlessness
bring a sort of tranquil beauty,
that makes you accept and nicely shrug
and sadly, sweetly smile?
Will I smile? Or will she?
Or will universal destruction take us both
together?
Then we will never have to face the lonely end.
Maybe this is why we want to blow ourselves
to kingdom come.

Oh my love, we must pass on some love.

And so we loved within these sheets,
where I sit within this familiar room,
under this universe; writing this.

Now she sleeps, lost in a book.
I will soon call her name, so as not to be
so lonely, And I shall say Erica
I want to read you something.
I shall call her name and this night will pass;
and so will so many,
and this world will pass and so will so many.
ERICA I WANT TO READ YOU SOMETHING.

1964

EXILE

It is raining outside.
It is raining.
The wet leaves are rotting into the earth,
into the sockets of my father's song,
into the mouth of my mother's skull
where she smiles for all eternity.

I am clutched by a cold sadness,
by loneliness, by loss.
Where do I belong?
I feel far away.
But far away from where?

It is raining outside;
far away from the wind on the hills
of my dream,
from the pipes and the birds of my song.

My son laughs in a strange language,
a language I understand too well.

Perhaps I should take my life and death
with me,
walk with my wife and my son and two
blankets,
into the rain.

1964

SORRY FOR THE NOISE — WE'RE DANCING

Who can that be?
I am expecting no-one.
I have heard the songs and psalms and sorrows
of lost boys on the path.

I wonder who on earth . . .?
I have seen the faces of this world
and settled by these walls
that sing with laughter.
Yet I jump when telephone calls,
but wait for a respectable three rings
before I answer.

HELLO?
YES! THIS IS ME!

I am here;
this is how I am
and how I shall always be.
HOW NICE TO HEAR YOUR VOICE AGAIN.

Nothing new will happen;
thank God for that.

REALLY!

My kids will grow up
and pass on the pain
I gave my father.

SORRY FOR THE NOISE. WE'RE DANCING.
I SAID SORRY FOR THE NOISE. WE HAPPEN TO BE DANCING.
HOW NICE! WHEN?

They will leave home and we will be gay
and cry.

Time will flow through this house
and silence.

WHEN? I'M NOT QUITE SURE WE CAN MAKE IT THEN.

From them I can expect pain.
Things that have happened will happen again.

SUNDAY WILL BE FINE. NO, I WON'T FORGET.

And we will pass the nights and dance the day
and expect no-one;
nothing but the inescapable future.
And we will watch sunsets
and feed birds.

YES, A PLEASANT SURPRISE. SEE YOU THEN.
GOODBYE.

I have heard the songs and the psalms and the sorrows,
left the lost boys on the path
and waved and looked away;
and felt the cold and the pain of my children,
seen the threatening sky and the rain
driving against the glass.
And the leaves gone
and the smoke of the leaves.
And I am expecting no-one
and I am glad.

1965

WARSAW PILGRIMAGE

Walls tremble through flame.
Child with no name,
hands up in the air.

The ghetto rubs its smokey paws
over Vistula.
Faces follow prayer into nowhere.

The wind has lost its voice tonight;
yet I hear a song
in a language long since dead.

They say they came with a brassband
the day after we died;
and played a Schubert serenade.

Boy with burning eyes
melting into the sky!
Girl, clutching down that cloud,

you are my very own
walls crumbling through flame.

Smoke of children with no name,
I am told I must forget you ever came.

1965

DIASPORA

How sad that I have found nowhere,
that I have found no dream,
that I come from nowhere and go nowhere.

This is a land without dream;
an endless landscape.

Beautiful for those who can see their own
sunset,
who can grow their own fruit out of their own
sweat.
Beautiful for those in their own land,
whose laughter, whose tears soak into their
own land.
Whose songs fill the earth and the sky of
their own land.

How beautiful to dance and move and live and
dream and die in a country with a dream.

How sad I am that I have found nowhere.
My tears fall into the brick and haste and
death of day to day existence.

This is a country without dream
and no-one notices that I am crying.
By the waters of my own four falling walls
I wail.
I hear the trumpets, see the invisible
machines of destruction working in every
corner.

How sad that I have found nowhere;
my son has no festival, this sun no ceremony.
How sad that the sea beyond does not lift me,
nor the hills.

1965

TO MY SON

My son, I have brought you into this;
into this world.
And I have never thought but loved.
Yet had I thought I would have done the same,
and I would never have you unborn,
and I have always loved your name,
since I threw my flame into another flame
and held you weeping when you came.

A girl and I and one night loving
dreamed and dredged you from the stars,
and up you came.
I loved your mother and I love her,
and I put you into her,
and now my love for her walks with you.

So be gentle in the night.

It is customary my son to tell you things;
to show you the way.
I who am lost and burning and trembling in the dark.

These words then are instead of words,
instead of tears.

So there you are; here.
Survivor from the night,
refugee from space. Smoke you are,
taken shape.
Beautiful child in the ghetto of your mind,
lost within the congregation of your shadows.

My son! You have your head, your heart, your soul,
your name, your fears, your face.
No-one can die your death or live your life.
We see you trying to take your place,
and search the questions that cloud your face,
we hear you singing with the worm,
we watch you struggling to conform.

And though your tears tear us apart
somewhere we are glad.

They can swim my son.
They can negotiate roads and sky and water
and rooms packed with people.
Falling in the garden does not cause them to drown.

Out of the window I see you all alone,
pursued by all of them.
But they do not see that you are pursued
by all the aeroplanes from within.
They do not hear your singing rabbis weeping
centuries of psalm and dust.
They do not smell these fearful faces of the past
who haunt you,
that cause the tears to fall along your lovely head.

Take care. Go through your way and come out
as you shall.
Out of your shell of troubled sleep.

I sing of times when these words have no meaning,
of a girl and you and one night loving;
who dream and dredge me up from dark.
Until then I hail you in your hell.
Become familiar with the stations of the star
so that you may truly enter out of pain.

And try to smile.

1966

NEW YEAR

This is the time to be alone,
with tinsel wrapped around my head,
listening to the living dead
hoot and cheer the year ahead.

And while you dream the clouds will clear
those fearful, restless years ahead.
You sleep this side of dancing wall
and ceiling shakes above our head.

This is the time to give my thanks
to telephone that does not ring.
I'll feed the fire and dance with glass,
and for myself and you I sing.

This is the time to congratulate
that sole celebrant in the glass,
and sit on floor and write these words
until the singing of the birds.

And now I come to softly stroke
you sleeping wife, and make you moan.
This is how I know I know
I am not so terribly alone.

My daughter sleeps in flesh of white
and Autumn has not touched her eyes.
She lives forever in her smile.
I close her door and scan the skies.

Now's the time for our newborn's feed;
I laugh and kiss her screaming head.
So fearful she will not be fed,
yet soon she sleeps so calm in bed.

And to another dark I'll creep
to watch my own son twist in sleep.
I'll weep within and shake my head
and smile as I touch his bed.

And then I'll slide into our bed
and hold you close til proper light.
I'll kiss and watch your sleeping head,
and stay awake all through this night.

Until our children wake and stretch,
and sing and dance and shout and yawn.
I'll keep the tinsel on my head,
until another year is born.

And they will share the tinsel out,
and press their noses against glass.
And we will watch them grow and grow
and go. And time will pass.

1966/67

PRAYER AT FORTY

There is this noise of silence
    as I enter my house;
and these children in attitudes
    of praying stone.
I cover them and they moan.

And there is this woman
in this room,
the girl who took my name
and breathed upon it.
There is this warm in my bed
when I touch and kiss her sleeping form.

        There is this you, miracled in the mirror.

I will go to bed.
I will close my head
and enter the dark flower of my wife.

You are a mirage in this desert.
I have drunk from you, sang songs beneath your cool limbs.

I climb into bed.

I had grown old wandering in this desert.
   My tongue had got thick and had gone mad and cursed God.
And I died.

But now I sing of marriage;
of love and work and marriage,
for only these exist.

Somewhere upon these impossible stairs
we are attempting love.
And the fire from our eyes may burn
   down this city.
For let us face it,
all in all we remain unearthed in North West Six.

Tomorrow we must wear disguise
and cry in tubes and turn away
from mumbled lives and the dumb
articulation of passers-by.

Dreaming one. Do you remember grass?
And walking through the orchards
of this metropolis?

Our children will soon awake.
Already I can hear the singing bird
in this black night.

They will rise and go up
   into the Jerusalem of tomorrow;
into the unborn lemon city of the heart;
into the soaring of arrows, the gathering
of flowers, and bread.

They must go up with their open eyes,
climbing the dust pyramids of our dead;
   and reach high enough to see
the fresh grass that breathes beyond,
and the unsmashed glass, and you and I.
And the bird with sun on throat and wing.

The limbs and the love and the laugh
of our children must go up and never die.

And we all will sing.

1967

WHATEVER HAPPENED TO ISAAC BABEL?

Whatever happened to Isaac Babel?
And if it comes to that —
whatever happened to those old men of Hackney
who sat around a wireless, weeping tears of pride
at weather forecasts from Radio Moscow?

Whatever happened to us? The Lovers of Peace?
And to our proud banners?
Whatever happened to our son?
And to that Picasso Dove of Peace
we brought back from Budapest?

Whatever happened to that little man
who tried to leap above himself?
He had a fire in his eyes;
a certain beauty in his eyes.
Or maybe that was merely poverty.

Whatever happened to Vladimir
Mayakovsky? Sergei Esenin? And Leon Trotsky?
Between the Instant Quaker and the Colour Supplement
we are apt to find no time to talk of them.

But then, we are apt to find no time to talk.

Now it is day,
and rather late in the day.
Whatever happened to us?

We are the worm contractors;
lusty youths of fire have become tweeded teachers,
with a swish Hi-fi that was bought for cash
and a smashing collection of Protest Songs.

O ye dreamers of peace!
Dreamers of a bright red dawn!
Whatever happened to that dream?

The dead are buried and the years
and forests of computers cover us.
We are crushed within the heart.
We are gone like prophet Leon
with ice-picks in our brain.

But there is no red stain.

We leave nothing behind
except volumes and volumes; such beautiful
volumes.
Unread but rather splendidly
displayed upon tasteful teak.

O ye sitters down for peace!
Only the pigeons protest
these days down Whitehall.
O Comrades of Slogan Square!
This is a windy Judas corner;
this is the fraught, frozen over winter park.

I smile and walk backward.
If you insist I am also part of this.
But through my clenched teeth
I somehow cannot stop myself chanting.

Whatever happened to Isaac Babel?
Whatever became of me?

I think often of Isaac Babel,
of his unsung death.
And as I walk away from you
I know that I am all full up.
I am all full up with people.
I have no vacancies.

Suicide at forty would be mere exhibitionism.

Besides, I have songs to sing.
Songs for myself;
songs to keep me warm;

songs to feed into mouths.
And I have one mouth in particular to kiss;
and eyes above that mouth from where I draw
my songs.
He was a funny little man, Isaac Babel.
And one would have thought him a nonentity,
had they not needed to dispose of him
so thoroughly in the dark.

Most people in this world are worthwhile;
therefore I can dispense with most of them.

You have to draw the line somewhere.

Yes, I think often of that little man
'with glasses on his nose and Autumn in his heart'.
Isaac Babel! Can you hear me?
I think often of your untelevised death.

Whatever happened to us
Returning from Whitehall
our banners smudged with rain,
our slogans running away?
Us waving, shaving, running after
our going youth and euphoria.
Hurtling through these fattening years
of hollow laughter.

And incidentally — who are we and
where are we?

So dreams die.
My dreams.
So can you blame me for building
barricades in West Hampstead?
Nice flat. Garden flat; un-numbered,
somewhere behind the Finchley Road.

With children laughing and children crying
and within me still one thread of longing.
And one wife calm and warm, belonging.

So — where was I?
Oh yes! Whatever happened to ——————?
What was his name?

Never mind, nothing really changes;
except children grow,
and we realise there is nowhere else to go.
There is only us now. Us alone.

And not forgetting that rather funny
little Jewish Cossack fellow
whose name at the moment slips the mind.
Not to worry, they're bound to know
in Better Books.

There is a certain joy in knowing;
but then again a certain peace and quiet in
half forgetting.

1967

CHILDREN

Who are these strangers come within these walls,
who now are fast asleep?
Their hands do not seem to need
to grasp or guard;
but are opened upward, palms towards the stars.
Why are they surrendering
when they have captured us?

1967

FOR THE RECORD

They came for him in Amsterdam; my grandfather David,
and with minimum force removed him from his house.

He surrendered to the entire German Army,
and that was that.

It is of little consequence now;
so many die alone in foreign lands.
But for the record I must say
they gave him a number, helped him
aboard an east-bound train.

It was a little overcrowded,
but then again they had so many to dispatch.

You might call him part of the biggest catch
in history of those who fish for men.

Anyway, to cut a long story short,
he was never seen again.

I cannot put my finger on the exact day he died.
Nor the time, nor the place.

Suffice to say it was by gas and in the east.

I write this merely to record the facts
for my descending strangers.

Furthermore, today is the 21st of December
in the year of our Lord 1968.
And it is getting rather late.
It rained this evening but now the wind has dropped
and the moon is shining.
It is 11.33 p.m. Precisely.

1968

SOMEWHERE OVER LONELY MEADOW

Somewhere over lonely meadow
where the wheat waits for the cut,
a silent exodus of swifts
sprinkle into dying sun.

Somewhere over lonely meadow
bats zigzag across the moon,
the dozing earth pulls down the sky
and opens trees when dead leaves fall.

Somewhere over lonely meadow
blackberries rotting on the bough,
remain unreached by fallen child
somewhere under lonely meadow.

Somewhere over lonely meadow
nothing changes all the time,
the chestnut ripens and the apple;
and the barking of a dog.

1969

QUESTIONS

What does your father do?
What does he do for a living?

He is a decomposer
and his eyes are open
twenty-four hours
of every every day.

What does your mother do?
What does she do for a living?

She is an earthwife.
And she lies beside him
forever and ever
and ever.

1970

NEW NOVEL

Last night my new book leapt high above itself.

And I can see it on the special shelf ——————

'—————— a novel of distinction. Elegant! An endless source
of wealth . . . . . . A master
piece, in my opinion.'

Would any critic now stand against so many
and dare deny my worth, and try to fight it?

All I've got to do now is try to write it.

1970

SUCCOT (HARVEST FESTIVAL)

Today we will go to Regent's Park
with our daughters and our son.
We will stand beneath a chestnut tree
and aim as high as clouds
for conkers.

Our laughter will rise into the sky
above those clouds, higher
than those other sounds
our children do not seem to hear.

Then, hungry we shall hurry home
and spread our harvest all around the floor,
and I suppose we shall sing
for songs are the dreams
we capture from the dark.

Meanwhile all this will have to suffice
for miracles.

1970

IVOR

My brother-in-law Ivor
wasn't a bad man.
Neither was he particularly good.
He was a big, busy fellow,
down to earth and hearty;
living beyond his means.

How are you Ivor? You would say.
How are things going?
Terrific! Fantastic! He would reply.
Couldn't be better old boy.

But everyone said as they shook their head,
Ivor, the way you live is suicide.

Anyway, to cut a long story short,
one day he died.

I never knew Ivor, the rabbi said.
But I believe he was a big man;
big in every way and loved by all.

Well, I don't know about that,
I murmured to myself in that cold bare hall
when prayers were read.

It was a most impressive funeral.
And so we followed Ivor,
slowly behind his coffin.
And when they lowered him
I smiled and I sighed,
and I laughed inside,
for Ivor,
who lived beyond his dreams,
whose life was suicide

I have met many good guys in my life.
So many nice chaps come and go,
yet I never remember them, like this.
Their faces coagulate; they are gone.

But I can tell you,
there was something about Ivor.

Whenever he entered a room it ignited into life.

1975

DIASPORA (II)

I live in West Hampstead
where happy children
of all ages play
in all languages.
No windows are broken here,
no graffiti.
All in all a pleasant place.
But fears creep in;
fears that drip at three
in the morning.
They rap on the door of my dream,
and there in the night
the windows of my synagogue
are shattered.

1975

ERICA BY LETHE

You wandered along the shore
considering the other side;
and I watched you, helpless.
There was nothing I could do
as I waited,
with all the nerve endings
of my love exposed;
unable, useless.
For the first time somehow at a loss.
You looked back at me,
your calm eyes floating above your pain,
as if weighing things up,
considering perhaps that I
would give you an even rougher ride
if you returned to us.

But it was for you to decide.

You chatted to the Boatman,
haggled for a while,
then suddenly you decided not to cross.

And so you came back to us, smiling.

1977

PASSOVER '38

One thing I remember
even more than the hunger.
Scrubbing my knees, smarting my hair and
rushing downstairs
into that playground of my childhood;
where all the other children
with their eyes alight
were building castles with crackernuts.

I built my castle.
I was a shopkeeper, a millionaire,
I ruled the world;
challenging all to chance
nuts of their own,
gathered from high pitched aunts
the day before,
as we went from home to home,
running that Yomtov gauntlet
of twisted cheeks and wet kisses.

In those days families extended forever and ever.

Who wants a castle?
Knock down my castle! I dared.
All in their sudden beauty
the girls came singing, flirting.
Holiday! Passover!
The Angel of Death? Who is he?
a madman on the radio, far away.

Passover lasted for the rest of the year;
the crackernuts secure
in the lining of my sleeve.
Belonging — we belonged.

Poverty came later,
when most of us did well
and moved away.

1980

THE FIRE NEXT TIME

Next time we are all in the box-car.
All on the fast track running out of control
towards our final destination.
Next time there will be no selection;
no survivors,
we will all be fodder for the great Moloch.
Next time there will be nothing left;
no-one.
No-one left to bear witness.
Next time, time itself is in the box-car,
Next time we are all on our way to the fire.

1980

OUR FRIEND SHIRLEY

Our friend Shirley lives just behind Swiss Cottage.
Her face is like a mobile, travelling round
and around the room, never still.
Her eyes are poised somewhere in that no-man's land
between joy and sorrow.
Eyes that have seen it all
yet still are not tired.
Eyes that have witnessed Europe's tragedy
and her own.
Our friend Shirley is a good girl.
Often she brings us Beigals from Grodzinski
when she comes to call.
Our friend Shirley lives alone,
works hard, tends her little back garden,
and never phones us with her troubles.

Except this evening.

"----- Guess what! You know that old girl,
the one who lives next door; the one I dress
every morning -------"

Yes. She had told us.
Every morning, before she goes to work,
our friend Shirley, out of love,
goes down into that basement and helps
that old girl into a little dignity.

"----- Guess what happened this morning?"

She died, I said.

"----- No, much worse. That old girl made
anti-Semitic remarks as I was dressing her.
She cursed the Jews; said they were the cause
of this country's troubles. She said the Jews
were in control -------"

What did you do? I said.

"----- Never said a word. I dressed her and
I left. And I'm never going back. She can rot
in her bed as far as I'm concerned.
Do you blame me?"

No! And as I put the phone down I wondered
how that old girl would manage tomorrow
morning, without our friend Shirley.

1983

FAMILY

Darling, let's have some babies I said.
That night you gave birth to all of them,
and each one laughed at seas of dark ahead.

Darling, let's have some children I said.
That day we danced with all four of them,
all were given names and clothed and fed.

Darling, let's have some human beings I said.
They went to school, we waved goodbye to them,
each walked away with a crisis in the head.

Darling, that was the family you said.
That night we cried and sang each one of them.
Alone and wonderful we went to bed.

1986

JESSICA

From the deserts of dark,
someone came to this oasis,
hungry for the milk of stars.
Given a name,
she now sleeps at the breast
of my daughter,
a piece of dreaming
sculpture.
Pale and perfect.
Only her mouth moves,
sucking sunlight.
The night dies.
Then suddenly she is becoming,
stirring, opening eyes.
And all at once she is alive,
is one of us.
She cries and cries.

You have to laugh.

1986

POOR OLD CROW

Note from nature article: *"Crow parents almost work themselves to death trying to feed their voracious young."*

I feel so close to crow.
I hover limp and ragged, croaking low.
I who sought the highest tree, so tired now;
I flap so slow. But I'll find the strength
to wave goodbye, for soon they'll go.
They'll leave poor crow,
poor thankful crow.
I'll sigh — Oh dear, must you go?
I'll cry.
I'll hide my wicked beady eye,
so full of glee.
I watch them practise flight,
day and night I hear them rise
and fall.
I've seen it all.
How terrible my children,
must you go? Must you leave old crow?
Oh soon I also want to go.
I want to fly away with lady crow.
I want some years of gluttony,
for me.

1986

MONDAY

How can I find inspiration
along the Finchley Road
at nine o'clock in the morning?
How can I laugh or cry, be moved,
be fired
by ravenous dustcarts
gobbling up empty boxes
of Kentucky Fried Chicken?
How can I find two words
to rub together?
Here somnambulists float
down into Underground,
programmed for another dreamless week.
And young girl mothers
most with their moist bloom
rubbed away,
disgorge their dreams at school gates.

1987

DAUGHTER, SON

Today the sadness of my daughter
was drowned in the laughter of my son.
She stood there on the shores of life,
silent and lost in the labyrinth of her eyes.
While my son sang of his exploits
on the other side of the world.
In joyous Wimbledon.
And all the time ravenous winter
swallowed light and night danced
with my daughter.
Slowly and slowly
the cymbal clouds
clapped hands and she cried
herself to sleep.
All night we lay awake, listening
to the storm, waiting for the dawn.
And in the dark, the sadness
of my daughter was drowned
by the crying of my son.
And we could hear her laughing
all the next day.

1987

WINTER SPRINGSONG

Winter the heavy breather
won't let go.
Peeking through the window,
creaking through the floorboards,
coughing through the walls,
howling through the corridors,
wheezing through the dark,
tapping with his white stick,
the old swine won't let go.
Go winter go!
You dirty old man,
hobble off, away with you,
We've had quite enough.
Haven't you heard the news?
We're dancing in this room,
as naked as our love;
as cheering as our song,
as fervent as our eyes,
as singing as our limbs,
as crazy as our hope.
Creep into a corner,
die and wither there,
as clouds unclothe the sun.

1987

DANCING PARTNER

Our thirty years have just sailed by;
we laugh and wave them come and go.
So lean on me and give me strength
and I'll forgive you all my sins.

1988

OUR KIDS HAVE JUST LEFT HOME

We sit here rather dazed:
our kids have just left home.
We gave them all our love,
they raided all our dreams
and ate up all our jam,
and left us just like that;
laughed all down the road.
Our kids have just left home.
And oh the sweet relief,
come, let's postpone our grief
and please answer the phone.

They're coming three oclock?
And staying for the night?
Where did we go right?

1988

FAX

Dear David,
good morning!
What is the weather like in Sydney?
Just to say that I am faxing
my kids over to you.
You will notice I am sending the originals,
but if you lose them not to worry.
We have copies.
They do have a few problems
but we are sure you can deal with them.
Thank you.

1988

SONGS FROM PLAYS

FLESHFIX

Are you feeling low or feeling hard?
All you need is cash or a banker's card.
It's fleshfix! Fleshfix!

We're all the same under the skin,
soon as we're out we want to get in.
It's fleshfix! Fleshfix!

It's the food of life, we want to give,
It's basic man, you need it to live.
It's fleshfix! Fleshfix!

Well hello Joe, do you wanna blow?
Well come inside, I'm ready to go.
It's fleshfix. Fleshfix!

Do you want clean French or hand relief?
You can stay all night or make it brief.
It's fleshfix! Fleshfix!

Or maybe all you want is a chat.
We'll take your money for providing that.
It's fleshfix! Fleshfix!

Do you want S & M or just play it straight?
We will always negotiate.
It's fleshfix! Fleshfix!

Come on friend, sex ain't no crime.
It's never early closing time.
It's fleshfix. Fleshfix!

You and I are both the same.
More or less we're all on the game.
It's fleshfix! Fleshfix!

LILY'S SONG

My name is Lily Framp,
I'm a first class filing clerk.
I keep myself to myself.
I work near St James's Park.
But I never stroll there after five;
Men are so beastly in the dark.

My superior is a lovely man.
He never interferes with me.
He keeps his hands to himself,
when I fetch him a cup of tea.
He shows remarkable self control,
considering he desires me.

I never did get married;
I have no time for men.
Their longing eyes caress my thighs.
They dream of endless sin.
Those horrid, ungracious,
slobbering, rapacious,
dirty sex-starved men.

You can feel their sexual yearnings,
when down telephones they call.
They haven't got a hope in hell,
for I shall never fall
into their filthy, lustful clutches
in the doorways of Whitehall.

Men are so hungry.
Men are so greedy.
Men are such gluttons in the dark.
In the dark. In the dark.

Oh my god, I mustn't think about it.

ZOE'S SONG

My dad. Wish he was dead.
Guess what he said?
Get into bed.
You thin little bitch,
you make my flesh twitch.
So he jumps into bed. My dad.

My dad. Wish he was dead.
Guess what he said?
Get out of bed.
You right little whore.
I'll smash in your jaw.
That's what he said. My dad.

My dad. Wish he was dead.
Guess what he said?
You're gone in the head.
Now get in your clothes.
Or I'll bite off your nose.
That's what he said. My dad.

My dad, Wish he was dead.
Guess what he said?
I'll puncture your lung
and gobble your tongue,
if you tell your mum.
That's what he said. My dad.

He gave me a quid.
That's what he did.
And poked out my eye
and kicked in my head.
I wish he was dead.
I wish he was dead.
Guess what he said?
Guess what he said?
Get out of bed.
Get into bed.
I got into bed.

Guess what he said?
Get out of bed.
You right little slut.
Now cover your cut
and keep your mouth shut.
That's what he said.
That's what he said.
I wish he was dead.
I wish he was dead.
My dad!

HOME

Home is where you rest your head.
Home is curling up in bed.
Home is where your parents wait.
Home is where you hang your hate.
Home is where they know your name.
Home is the drudge your mother became.
Home is where you all grow old.
Home is the place where love went cold.

CATS

They stare from windows with eyes of hate;
in every room they watch and wait;
in every city, so smugly curled.
Cats are awaiting to take over the world.

1988

SELF DESTRUCT

It was one of those days
when I was very angry with the universe.
I took my underarm stink eradicator
and aimed it at the stars.
"To hell with the ozone layer!
Get lost god!
Start somewhere else!"

1988

AND PEACE WILL COME

and peace will come and the living
men will go
and snow will fall upon the snow
and they will say they
did not die in vain

and another war and another
war will come again
and again and
the living men and the living
men will go and fall
asleep and cover them
with again and snow and
peace will come and all who move
or breathe will come and go
and come and go like leaves and
leaves of centuries of snow
will fall and fall

and peace and war will come
and go and go and come
and cover all and snow
and snow and snow and wind and rain
and snow will fall upon the snow
and peace will come and everyone
will know they did not go in vain

and another sky will die
and come and go again and again
and again
and again
and peace will come

1970